THE SPARK

A GLIMPSE TO THE ELECTRICALS

G. L. JAI PURUSHOTHAM RAJ

ISBN 979-888606789-7

Contents

Preface

The opportunities for learning things have been broadened because of the internet and social media. Students are learning and updating themselves with a lot of new things apart from learning from their educational institutions. But there are also a few challenges in this modernization. The exploration is drastically reduced because of the present circumstances. It is good to have an education with the new technologies, but exploration is needed for the education. Because of the lack of exploration, the present generation is lagging with the interest to study things. Because of the lagging of interest, the students have forgotten their correct destiny. Even though we have 'n' number of opportunities to learn new things from the internet and social media, this exploration and the interest can only be created from teachers and proper books. There is a proverb called "Old is Gold". Our traditional method of reading books is the only way to regain our exploration. The intention of this book is to create interest towards electricals, and also to encourage in reading books and learning things properly from teachers. This book was not created with any pre-planned ideas. It is just a fusion of my basic thoughts and knowledge in the field of electrical engineering.

I sincerely express my gratitude to Assistant Professor Mr. D. Citharthan of Christ The King Engineering College for introducing me to this

Notion Press Platform and giving me confidence in writing this book. I would like to thank our Head of the Department for EEE, Dr. M. Arumuga Babu, and Principal Dr. M. Jeyakumar of Christ The King Engineering College for supporting and encouraging students like me to enhance our additional skills. I would also like to thank our Reverence Father John Britto and the management of Christ The King Engineering College for giving this wonderful space to us to explore and learn new things.

G. L. Jai Purushotham Raj

CHAPTER ONE

INTRODUCTION

"THE SPARK" literally enlightened the world. When an ancient man rubbed two stones, coincidently he observed a spark while rubbing those stones. If he had not witnessed that spark, then probably we could not have discovered the fire and the following. While seeing that spark from the stones, he got a spark within him. There started the evolution.

Once there lived a boy named Yash.

He was a good learner. He has completed his 12th standard and scored high marks. As a result of his hard work, he got a seat in IIT Delhi for Electrical and Electronics Engineering. His parents were very happy, but he was not happy because he was not interested in Electrical Engineering.

He really doesn't know about his future.

But, this was his parent's dream. His parents were interested to give him a high esteemed education to him. Yash loved his parents. So, he was not willing to be a barrier to their happiness and accepted to join IIT without interest.

The day came. Yash arrived at the train and the train started towards Delhi. He was in a confused state. He doesn't know how this train travel is going to change his life.

A person came and sat next to Yash on the train. Yash was not in a mood to see and communicate with any people. The person sitting next to Yash smiled at him. Yash responded to him with a sad smile. Yash doesn't know that the person sitting next to him was a college professor. That professor started his conversation with Yash.

PROFESSOR: Hi, may I know your good name, please?

YASH: Hello Sir, my name is Yash.

PROFESSOR: Nice to meet you. Are you studying?

YASH: No Sir, I am speaking with you.

PROFESSOR: (laughed) No, I have asked you whether you are studying in a school or college.

YASH: I have completed my 12th standard. I got a seat in IIT Delhi for Electrical and Electronics Engineering. That's why I am going to Delhi.

PROFESSOR: Oh! congrats.

YASH: No thanks Sir.

PROFESSOR: Why are you so sad my boy? Are you not interested in your studies.

YASH: Actually, I don't have an interest in engineering, especially in electrical engineering.

PROFESSOR: Why? Any hatred towards electricals?

YASH: I don't know why. I couldn't understand the basic concepts of electrical engineering from my *school days. That's why I don't like it. But for the sake of my parents, I am going to Delhi. It is definitely not for myself.*

PROFESSOR: I can understand your feeling. I will help you to get out of this problem.

YASH: But how? Are you going to speak to my parents regarding this?

PROFESSOR: (laughed) No my child. I will give you an outline about electrical engineering so that, you might understand something about it.

YASH: Oh! Ok, but, how do you know about electricals?

PROFESSOR: I am also an electrical engineer working as a professor.

YASH: Oh! nice to meet you, Sir. But, do you think I can understand the concepts?

PROFESSOR: Why not! I believe in you. But the thing is, I couldn't take a lecture here with the black board as we are in the train now. I also didn't bring any pen and paper to explain the concepts. I will just explain you some of the concepts randomly about electricals. You can visualize it by yourself. I will try my level best to make you understand the glimpse of the electricals. The rest is up to you.

YASH: Anyway, it is a train travel. This is my seat. I couldn't jump halfway from the running train. Instead of sleeping alone, I can hear your story and try to understand something.

PROFESSOR: Don't worry. Be confident. I will try to trigger your interest in electricals

CHAPTER TWO

ELECTRIC CHARGE

PROFESSOR: If you need to construct a building, the basement is very important. Like that, in electrical engineering, we need to know about the basement. So firstly, I am going to explain to you about electric charge.

Just like objects can have mass, temperature, or speed, objects can also have charge. It is just a property. Things like ballon or hair become charged by transferring electrons.

Inside atoms, protons and neutrons are the heavier particles and the electron is the lightest particle. The protons and neutrons will be at the center of the atom and the electrons will be at the outside.

For eg:- If we rub a balloon against someone's hair, the balloon and the hair attract each other.

YASH: I have one doubt sir.

PROFESSOR: Yes!!

YASH: Can we say that the hair which is rubbed against the ballon is having some gravity?

PROFESSOR: Theoretically, there are a lot of similarities between Newton's Law of Gravity and Columb's Law of Electricity.

The ballon which was rubbed against the hair gained electrons from the hair. So, the ballon is negatively charged and the hair becomes positively charged. So, they are what can be gained or lost when things rub against each other.

Thus the charge is bipolar, meaning that electrical effects are described in terms of positive and negative charges. But they are just like labels. It is just to show that, these two types show opposite behaviors. The labels we use today were decided 270 years ago in 1748 by Mr. Benjamin Franklin. The basics are that opposite charges attract each other and the like charges repel each other.

PROFESSOR: Now, I understand that you will be having doubts. Just hold it. The next content we are going to see is the chain to this concept.

YASH: Ok Sir.

CHAPTER THREE

ELECTRIC CURRENT

Now, let us consider the electric charge. A unique feature of electric charge is that it can be transferred from one place to another. This motion of charges from one place to another creates an electric field. This movement of charges creates an electric current.

YASH: Sorry for the interruption Sir

PROFESSOR: Yes

YASH: You have said that movement of charges creates current. Then can we say that the electric current is due to the flow of both the protons and electrons as both are charged particles?

PROFESSOR: *Ok, for this question, I would like to say further about charges so that, you can easily understand the solution for this doubt.*

Electric Charge is the physical property of subatomic particles like electrons, protons, and neutrons. We know that electron is a negatively charged particle, a proton is positively charged and the neutron is zero charged. The neutron has an equal amount of positive and negative charges in it. That's why neutrons have zero charges. Protons and neutrons combined to form a nucleus which is at the center of the atom and the electrons revolve around the nucleus.

In solids, the nuclei are strongly bonded with the adjacent atoms to make the rigid structure. Hence the protons are not movable in solids. But, we can move electrons easily by giving sufficient energy.

PROFESSOR: *So, that is the reason for which, the electric current is due to the flow of electrons only.*

Now, we can define current as "The amount of charge passing through the cross-section of a conductor in 1 second. It can also be defined as the rate of charge flow.

YASH: Yes Sir. Now, I am clear with the concept of electric current. But what does AC and DC Current mean Sir?

PROFESSOR: It is a very deep concept. But still, I will give you an outline of it.

When a current is constant with time, we say that we have a direct current. Thus a DC Current is one that remains constant with time.

On the other hand, a current that varies with time, reversing its direction periodically is called an AC or Alternating Current.

YASH: What is the direction of current flow, Sir?

PROFESSOR: Actually, the flow of electrons is from the -ve to the +ve terminal.

But theoretically, the current direction is mentioned from +ve to -ve terminal. It is because, at the time of the discovery of electricity, the electron was not yet discovered. So, in previous days, scientists thought that current flows from the +ve terminal to the -ve terminal. Even after the discovery of electrons, this notation was not updated.

YASH: Ok Sir. I can understand this. One more doubt for me. This is my long-time doubt for me. So, I will ask for it with your permission.

PROFESSOR: Yes proceed.

YASH: Sir, Why AC Supply is given to our homes? Can DC Supply be given to our homes? If not, why?

PROFESSOR: *To answer this question, I would like to tell you a story.*

At the time of the invention of currents, there was a big war of currents whether to use AC current or to use DC Current in our home. The war was between Thomas Alva Edison and Nicolas Tesla. Edison preferred DC current to be used in our home whereas, Tesla suggested AC currents to be used in our home. It was a current war during that period.

Edison claimed strongly that the AC current was more dangerous than the DC current. He conducted many experiments regarding this and tried to prove his point.

Later after a few years, American Government had planned to generate electricity from the Niagra River. But they had a confusion that which kind of power to generate whether DC or AC. Edison suggested DC to the government whereas Tesla suggested AC to the government. After a long discussion, the American government has finally approved to generate AC current.

YASH: But, why? Why do they have preferred AC current?

PROFESSOR: Because it is easier to distribute the AC current over long distances with relatively low losses.

YASH: Sir, can you please explain this in detail?

PROFESSOR: Sure!

AC is used in most electricity distribution systems for several reasons. But the most important thing is the ease with which, it can be transformed from one voltage to another. But for DC, it is more difficult to get transformed from one voltage to another. The energy losses will be low in AC than DC during the transmission. There is also another reason. But, before that, we will recall about DC and AC. Now, do you know the difference between AC and DC?

YASH: Yes Sir. DC means Direct Current which will be constant with respect to time. AC means Alternating Current which will be varying with respect to time. Varying means, the amplitude will be from positive to zero, then zero to negative, then negative to zero, and from zero to positive. This cycle keeps on continues.

PROFESSOR: Literally, an impressive explanation. You have almost said the answer

Now, You just imagine, you are giving 230 V DC supply to one house after considering all the losses. If some electric shock tends to happen to a person in that house, the current will be constant and continuous and it may lead to death at a very short period of time because of that constant current along with the 230 V.

If you take an AC Supply, if an electric shock happens to a person, the current passing through him will be alternated in nature. So, the current value is varying. At some point, the amplitude of the current with respect to time will come to negative and zero. We can now say that the impact of the electric shock will be lesser in AC compared to DC.

CHAPTER FOUR

VOLTAGE

YASH: Sir, from my school days, I am unclear about the concept of voltage. Can you please explain about voltage Sir?

PROFESSOR: Sure, I would like to explain this through an experiment.

Imagine you have two beakers filled with water in equal amounts. Let us name the beakers as beaker 1 and beaker 2. These two beakers are connected through a pipe.

If we observe the two beakers for a few seconds, do you think the water will flow from one beaker to another?

YASH: As a pipe is connected between two beakers, I think, the water will flow from one beaker to another

PROFESSOR: But, it is not correct. I will tell you the reason

As both Beaker 1 and Beaker 2 have the same amount of water, there will be no water flow from one beaker to another beaker.

Now, let me give you a task. Without changing the amount of water in any of the beakers, can you make the water flow from one beaker to another?

YASH: Can you please repeat the question once again Sir?

PROFESSOR: Understand my question again. You need to make the water flow from beaker 2 to beaker 1. But, you are not allowed to change the amount of water in any of the beakers. So, you can't add or remove the water from any of the beakers. How will you do it?

YASH: Puzzling question. I couldn't guess the answer. Please tell me the answer, Sir.

PROFESSOR: It is so easy.

One of the things you can do is, you can raise the height. You can raise the height of beaker 2, so that, the water will flow from beaker 2 to beaker 1. Now, the height difference causes the water to flow from beaker 2 to beaker 1

In an exactly similar way, for electricity to flow, there must be a factor like height for this beaker experiment. Before seeing about that, I will ask you one question.

We have a single copper wire with us without any circuit connections. Do you think the current will flow through the copper wire?

YASH: I think, the current will flow

PROFESSOR: Yes, copper is a good conductor of electricity. But, electricity will not flow through a simple copper wire because nothing is triggering it. The factor that triggers the copper wire to conduct electricity is called the potential difference or the voltage

YASH: Oh! That's great. But, can you explain this much deeper as it is a very important topic in electrical engineering?

PROFESSOR: Sure, let us dive a bit deeper into this concept. Are you aware of the word potential?

YASH: Yes Sir!

PROFESSOR: Where did you study about this?

YASH: In physics, I have learned about potential energy

PROFESSOR: Can you say about it

YASH: It is the stored energy when the object is at rest

PROFESSOR: A precise one! But, we will study this concept with an example

When you are holding a ball in your hand, it has some potential energy. When you drop it, the potential energy gets converted into kinetic energy. When the object is in motion, the object is said to have kinetic energy.

Now, the ball in our hand has high potential energy and the dropped ball have low potential energy. Similar to that, a negative charge close to the negative charges has high potential energy. If left free, the negative charge will be repelled by other negative charges and move towards the positive charge which has low potential energy.

The potential difference is the difference in the electrical pressure between the two points. Potential difference is also referred to as voltage. Voltage can be defined as the work done to move a unit charge from one point to another.

YASH: *Yes Sir, Now I can able to understand this. But, are voltage and EMF are same?*

PROFESSOR: *This is another common doubt among all. Even I had this doubt during my college days. We will see about it*

Many people will think that voltage and EMF are the same. But, there is indeed a difference between voltage and EMF. To understand the difference between the voltage and the emf, let's experiment.

Let us assume we are having two bottles filled with water, namely Bottle A and Bottle B. Bottle A is having more water and Bottle B is having less water. Technically we can say that bottle A is having a higher potential of 10 V whereas bottle B is having a lower potential of 4 V. We will connect both the bottles with a pipe. As we pour water to bottle A, the water flows from bottle A to bottle B through a pipe. That is, we can say that the electrons flow from higher potential to lower potential.

Water is flowing from one bottle to another because there is a difference in the water level of both bottles. Similarly, we can say that as potential difference or voltage. Thus, we can define potential difference or voltage as one, which is needed to make the electrons flow from one point to another.

This water flow between these two bottles continues, until the difference in water flow exist. If two water levels become equal, then there won't be any water flow between bottle A and bottle B.

For the continuous flow of water between the two bottles, let us connect a device that again and again creates a difference in the water level of two bottles, so, there will be continuous water flow between two bottles. This is called an EMF.

So, with this experiment, we can say that the potential difference or voltage is what makes the electron flow in the circuit and EMF maintains that potential difference or voltage.

YASH: I can understand the difference between the EMF and the voltage now Sir. I would like to ask you one more doubt with your permission.

PROFESSOR: Yes

YASH: You have explained to me about current and voltage. Now, Which one is dangerous? A high current or a high voltage?

PROFESSOR: Ok, for this, I would like to explain to you with an example.

Imagine a man A with a big sword in his hand. But, he hits you with the sword very softly. A man B is having a small pin and hits you with that small pin very hardly. Now, which will be more painful to you?

YASH: The man hitting me with a small pin will be very painful.

PROFESSOR: But the sword is bigger than the pin in size right. Then why can't the sword hurt you much harder than the pin in this case?

YASH: Sir because the pin hit me more forcefully than the sword.

PROFESSOR: That's my point. You consider this bigger sword as a high current and this small pin as a low current. When the high current has low voltage, that is less force, then the high current is less dangerous. When the low current has high voltage, that is high force, then that low current becomes dangerous because of the high voltage associated with it. So, according to me, high voltage is more dangerous than high current. But the combination of the high current and the high voltage becomes even more dangerous.

CHAPTER FIVE

CONDUCTORS AND INSULATORS

PROFESSOR: Ok now, have you heard about conductors and insulators?

YASH: Yes Sir, I have learned about this in physics. But, I forget about it now.

PROFESSOR: Ok, I will explain this topic. This topic is very important in electrical engineering. Now, What do you understand by the term 'Conduct'?

YASH: To transfer something?

PROFESSOR: Exactly!

A material that transfers something from one place to another is called a Conductors. Now, we can define electrical conductors as the materials that transfer electricity through them. I would like to explain this with an example.

We will connect the bulb to the battery with the help of the wire. The bulb will glow because of that copper wire. This copper wire is called the conductor because it conducts electricity.

If we connect the bulb and the battery with the thread, the bulb will not glow because of the thread. This thread is called an insulator because it does not transfer electricity.

YASH: Now, I have a doubt, Sir. You have said that the material which conducts electricity is called Conductors. Generally, we are capable of getting electric shock. Then, can we say that humans are conductors?

PROFESSOR: Good thinking. Your perception is correct. Humans are generally good conductors of electricity. This is the reason we used to get an electric shock when we are not careful.

YASH: If a person is getting an electric shock, how can we save him, Sir?

PROFESSOR: This time, you try to guess the answer.

YASH: Ok. I will try to push or pull the person who is getting an electric shock.

PROFESSOR: If you do like that, then you will also get the electric shock.

YASH: But, how Sir?

PROFESSOR: As I already said to you that humans are good conductors of electricity. So, If you touch the person who was getting an electric shock, You will also get that electric shock since you are also a conductor.

YASH: Then, how can we save him, Sir?

PROFESSOR: You can use wood.

Wood is a very good insulator. With the wood, You can hit the place smoothly where he is in contact with that electrical entity. As wood is an insulator, it resists the flow of electricity, and thus, he can be saved from the electric shock.

YASH: Sir, there was my friend. He is no more now.

PROFESSOR: I am so sorry.

YASH: It's ok Sir. While speaking about this topic, I suddenly had his thought in my mind. He died because of electric shock. This has happened

He was ironing his clothes with the help of an electric iron box. He was wearing a copper band in his hand. That copper band suddenly contacted the electric iron box and he had an electric shock. I heard that he became unconscious because of that electric shock. But, he died because of that electric shock. I still couldn't able to realize the reason for his death. Why Sir? Why does this need to happen to my friend?

PROFESSOR: First of all, I regret this incident. Yash, as I said to you before that copper is a good conductor of electricity. As the copper band tend to contact the electric iron box, which leads to electric shock.

YASH: Yes Sir. I can able to understand that because of this conductivity concept you have thought me now.

PROFESSOR: Yes. I would like to explain this conceptually.

In cartoons, it is pretty easy to tell when somebody is getting electric shock. Their skeleton flashes through their skin, their hair sticks straight up and there is smoke everywhere, maybe some electric sparks radiating out from the body.

YASH: Yes Sir. In cartoons, I have noticed these things and used to laugh hard, since I don't know the seriousness of this at a small age.

PROFESSOR: Ok,

But, what happens when someone is getting electric shock is much less flashy and much more dangerous.

Technically, we call this electric shock electrocution. It is the electric current running through the body. It comes from the combination of the words "Electric" and "Execution". So, it was specifically combined to describe the death by the electric shock. Whether an electric shock becomes electrocution depends on the nature of the current involved.

We already know that the current is the flow of the electric charge carried by electrons or ions and our bodies are pretty responsive to them because they use current at all time.

YASH: But how our bodies use currents all time Sir?

PROFESSOR: Good question.

Our bodies use current all time. For eg: tiny electric pulses from the movement of ions across membranes are what trigger neurons, which allow me to move and to be alive and make me talk to you right now.

So when you got an electric shock or a much stronger current passes through your body, the tissues overreact to that electricity.

The amount of current that is flowing is measured in ampere and a current of only 20 milli Ampere can cause someone to lose control of the diaphragm and stop breathing. 100 mill Ampere of current can stop a heart.

YASH: Oh! My god.

PROFESSOR: Yes, it is that much serious.

Now, this is all about the electric shock. And you have also asked me another question about the reason for his death. I will explain to you my understanding of it.

You have told me that your friend became unconscious for a while. At that time, his heart may fail to function for a while. Before calling an ambulance, a first aid method is there to overcome this problem. It is called CPR.

YASH: CPR? What is it, Sir?

PROFESSOR: CPR stands for CARDIOPULMONARY RESUSCITATION.

As his heart stops pumping suddenly, the breathing also gets stopped. The blood circulation to the brain also gets stopped. Because of this, it may lead to death, if there is any delay to resume the functioning of the heart. To avoid such a situation, A person must be given first aid attention. CPR is a first-aid technique that can save lives in such situations if performed correctly. It doesn't need any special kind of equipment. Your hands are enough for performing CPR. I can say you orally about it now, but, it will not be correct. I have said you the purpose of the CPR. Now, you need to learn about CPR and its techniques under the guidance of doctors.

YASH: Sadly, we couldn't save my friend's life. But, I will not let this happen again to anyone. I take an oath that I will definitely learn about CPR and also, I will create awareness about this to people.

PROFESSOR: That's my boy!

CHAPTER SIX

OHM'S LAW

PROFESSOR: Now, I will teach you the important concept called Ohm's law. In electrical engineering, there are many laws, but, as you are a fresher, you must have good knowledge in the Ohm's Law.

YASH: Yes Sir. I have learned somehow about it. But, I am eagerly waiting for your explanation Sir.

PROFESSOR: Yes.

Now for this, I will take two beakers. Let us keep Beaker A and Beaker B.

YASH: Sir, it is boring to keep the names like A and B. Shall we change the names now.

PROFESSOR: Ok, it's up to your choice now.

YASH: Now, I will name it Beaker Jil and Beaker Juk.

PROFESSOR: Not bad. Ok, now let us take Beaker Jil and Beaker Juk.

These two beakers were filled with water in equal levels. Both the beakers were connected with the pipe. Now, we are placing the beaker Juk above the height of the beaker Jil. Now, what happens?

YASH: The water now will be flowing from the beaker Juk to the Beaker Jil.

PROFESSOR: Exactly.

Now, listen carefully. If you understand this, you will understand Ohm's law too.

As we discussed, it is the height difference that makes the water flow from the beaker Juk to the beaker Jil. If we further increase the height, the flow of water will be even faster.

Now we can say that flow of water is directly proportional to the height difference.

Let us look at the other factor, how thin the pipe is. When the pipe becomes thinner, the water flow becomes slow.

Thinner the pipe, slower the flow of water. So, now we can say that the water flow is inversely proportional to the thinness of the pipe. Finally, we can say that flow of water is directly proportional to the height difference of the beakers and inversely proportional to the thinness of the pipe.

Remember this example because it is analogous to Ohm's Law. The flow of water is analogous to the flow of current. The height difference is analogous to the voltage and the thinness is analogous to the resistance. Thus now, we can say that the flow of current is directly proportional to the potential difference between the points and inversely proportional to the resistance. If the voltage is more, the current flowing will be more. If the resistance is more, the current flow will be less.

YASH: Yes Sir, I am clear with this concept now Sir.

MAGNETIC EFFECTS OF ELECTRIC CURRENT

YASH: *Sir, I have learned that electric current has some magnetic effects. But how does it happen, Sir? How electricity and magnetic effects are interrelated?*

PROFESSOR: *Actually, there is a subject called Electromagnetic theory, which deals with this concept. But to make it simple for you to understand, I will try to explain you as clear as possible. You just take that as a spark and learn further.*

YASH: Ok Sir.

PROFESSOR: First of all, we will discuss the basics of the magnetic effect.

Now, let us take a bar magnet, which has two poles namely the North pole and the South pole. You are bringing an Iron nail close to that bar magnet. What will happen?

YASH: The iron nail and the bar magnet will get attracted to each other.

PROFESSOR: Yes.

But, have you thought, why does an iron nail stick to the magnet? This is because of the force of attraction that binds the bar magnet and the iron nail together. This force is called the magnetic force.

Now, I would like to ask you one interesting question to you. Is magnetic force a contact force? In other words, is there a contact necessary between the bar magnet and the iron nail for the magnet to attract the nail?

YASH: I think it will be a contact force. Because it is getting attracted because of bringing both the iron nail and the bar magnet closer.

PROFESSOR: But, it is not correct. I will tell you the reason.

If you bring the iron nail slowly towards the magnet, at some point, the magnet also moves towards the nail. It means that the force came into action even there was no contact between the iron nail and the magnet. Thus, from this, we can say that the magnetic force is a non-contact force.

This magnetic force tells us that, there is an invisible field produced by the magnet in the space around it. We cannot see this field, but it exists. This field is produced by a magnet and hence it is called a magnetic field.

The magnetic field closer to the magnet is called the strong magnetic field and the magnetic field away from the magnet is called the weak magnetic field.

There are two types of magnets namely temporary magnets and permanent magnets. A temporary magnet retains magnetism for a very short period. A permanent magnet retains magnetism for a very long time.

We already know that like poles repel each other and unlike poles attract each other. This property is called magnetism.

Now, the process through which any non-magnetic object acquires magnetism is called as Magnetization process.

YASH: Oh! Is it possible to make a non-magnetic object into a magnetic object?

PROFESSOR: Yes. With the magnetization process, it is possible.

In 1819, there was a scientist namely Hans Christian Oersted. He found out that, if you keep a compass near a current-carrying conductor, then the compass needle deflects to some extent.

Now, we can say that, as the current flows through the wire, it produces a magnetic field around the wire. In other words, we can say that the wire becomes a temporary magnet while carrying an electric current. This is the reason for the deflection of the compass needle when we bring it near the current-carrying wire.

CHAPTER EIGHT

IMPORTANCE OF FUSE

YASH: Sir, I have heard that it is dangerous to have a short circuit because it causes damage to the electrical appliances in our home. But, if by mistake, if there is a short circuit in our home, then how will we protect the electrical appliances from being damaged?

PROFESSOR: I will explain to you about this.

Everything in the world needs protection. This becomes a mandatory thing. Similarly, every electric circuit needs protection from the overcurrent.

When an electric current is passed through the conductor, a small voltage drop is created across the conductor and some power is dissipated as heat. If the current increases, the heat generated also increases. In this case, do you know what happens, if the temperature increases? Now let us see this with an example.

Ice melts as the temperature increases. The same thing happens to the conductor. When the temperature increases beyond the threshold point, the conductor melts. Now, this is the basic principle behind the electric fuse.

YASH: Fuse?? Do you mean Nuclear Fusion?

PROFESSOR: No my child, I will tell you about it.

An electric fuse is a safety device, that has a melted wire within it, which melts when the temperature becomes high. This metal is made of Zinc, Copper, Silver, Aluminium, or other alloys.

YASH: Sir, but how this fuse protects our circuit?

PROFESSOR: Yes, I will explain to you.

This electric fuse is connected in series with the circuit to be protected. So, the current flowing through the electric circuit and the fuse will be the same. So, when the overcurrent flows through the metal in the electric fuse melts, the circuit is disconnected from the source.

Thus the fuse protects the circuit from the overcurrent by sacrificing itself.

YASH: It is a great invention as it helps us to protect the circuit and the electric appliances.

PROFESSOR: Yes.

Today, we have different types of fuses such as a rewirable fuse, Automotive fuse, Dry out fuse, Resettable fuse, Semiconductor fuse, Switch fuse, and Cartridge fuse.

The most commonly used fuse is the rewirable fuse. They are simple fuse used in our homes and offices. They usually consist of a carrier and a socket. When a fuse wire melts, the carrier is taken out. The melted wire is replaced by a new metal wire and it is put back into the circuit for the normal operation.

We have to be very careful while selecting a fuse for our circuit because, if we select the wrong fuse, safety is not ensured.

YASH: Sir, what is the process involved in selecting a fuse?

PROFESSOR: It is very simple.

For example, if we use a fuse wire that melts at 10 Ampere, which is connected with the circuit that operates at 12 Ampere, then what happens?

This fuse will melt even at a normal operating current. So, while choosing the fuse, the current rating of the fuse must be greater than the normal operating current of the circuit.

Similarly, when a short circuit occurs, an overcurrent flows through the circuit, then the fuse wire should melt safely, without any fire, breakage, or explosion. Therefore breaking capacity of the fuse must be greater than the short circuit current.

Another important factor is to be considered while selecting a fuse is speed. The speed at which the fuse wire melts depends on the metal at which the metal wire is made.

A circuit requires an ultrafast fuse, as it heats rapidly when excess current flows. Similarly, a time-delay fuse can be used to protect the equipment like a motor.

PROFESSOR: Now, one question. Can we use the same fuse for the DC and AC circuits?

YASH: *Maybe it can be used.*

PROFESSOR: *But the answer is no.*

Because, as we have already discussed that, an AC, the magnitude of the current will become zero many times. Zero currents are very easy for the melting fuse to stop.

Whereas in DC, the magnitude of the current never becomes zero. Also, the fuse has to take full responsibility with no help from the current. So, we will use a separate fuse for DC. A DC fuse is more complex and we will be using more elements in it.

YASH: *Sir, In my home, I have MCB. I heard that it protects our home from the short circuits. But how?*

PROFESSOR: MCB stands for Miniature Circuit Breaker. This is a big concept. But, I will try to explain it precisely to you. You will learn about this in our future subjects.

A tiny interesting device called MCB protects us and our homes from electrical mishaps. These breakers save us from two situations. The first is short circuit and the second is overload conditions.

In a short circuit condition, the MCB trips or breaks in 3 milliseconds and isolates the internal connections.

The fuse which we have seen previously is used in earlier days for our home protection. Now, we started using MCB for our home protection.

YASH: Yes Sir. I can understand these basics. Now, because of you, I got interested in learning about MCB further.

PROFESSOR: Good. You must learn further about this as we are using this in our day to day life.

52

CHAPTER NINE

TURNING TRAFFIC INTO ELECTRICITY

PROFESSOR: As we are speaking more about the subject, you might get bored. So, let us talk about some interesting topics in electrical engineering.

YASH: Interesting! It's my pleasure to hear from you.

PROFESSOR: I will share the information, well actually, this information was new to me a few years ago. I got amazed while knowing about this information and I am glad to share this with you.

In 2008, the East Japan Railway Company installed a floor at Tokyo station that generates electricity every time a person steps on it. They use this generated electricity to operate ticket gates and display systems.

YASH: Wow! That sounds great.

PROFESSOR: Yes.

The same technology is used in a club in San Francisco. They used this technology on their dancing floor to power the lights.

Now, it seems this floor generates electricity when it experiences some pressure.

Scientists took this technology to the next level. They thought, it would be good if they install this on a busy road, where it can experience constant pressure from the moving road vehicles. Now, you might be curious about this magical floor right.

YASH: Absolutely Sir! I have never heard like this in my life. I am curious to know about this Sir.

PROFESSOR: Yes.

Before learning about the mystery behind the floor, let us learn about the interesting physics concept called the Piezoelectric effect.

In 1880, Jacques Curie along with his younger brother Pierre Curie found that, when they hit certain types of crystals including Quartz, Tourmaline, and Rochelle Salt, along with certain axes, a voltage was produced on the surface of the crystal.

Generally, crystals are defined by their organized arrangement of atoms in a repeating pattern. This repeating unit is called the Unit cell.

In most crystals, the atoms in their unit cells are distributed symmetrically around a center point. Some crystalline material doesn't possess this center of symmetry making them candidates for piezoelectricity. Not all Non-Centrosymmetric crystals are piezoelectric materials. They might be symmetric, but they are electrically neutral, which means, they have an equal number of positive and negative charges.

Now, if we apply mechanic pressure, the structure deforms, atoms get pushed around, pushing the negative charge to one side and the positive charge to the other side.

Now, this crystal acts as a kind of a tiny battery, with the positive charge on the one face and the negative charge on the opposite face. Now, the current flows if we connect two faces to make a circuit.

YASH: Oh! Ok, Sir. But, how they will be practically placed under the road?

PROFESSOR: I will tell you.

Now, what if we bury crystals under city streets to capture energy as cars and people pass by?

The crystal is placed 5 cm below the surface of the asphalt. The asphalt is elastic, and the pressure of each tire or foot that passes it slightly deforms the crystal thereby producing electricity. Here, the electricity is generated from the vehicle's weight, motion, and vibrations. The produced electricity can be stored in a battery or it can be connected to a grid. The generated electricity could be used to power the street lamps, traffic signals, and car charging stations.

If planted along one kilometer stretch of road, an average of 400 KW of power can be generated. The busy roads and the heavy vehicles produce more electricity.

And also, piezoelectric material lasts for at least 30 years, which has more life than the life of the roads. It can also be used in the railways and airline runways.

YASH: It is a great discovery in the modern era of mankind. Almost our world is fully covered with roads and railway tracks. The maximum usage is there in this. If we generate electricity from this, we can fight against the scarcity of the electricity in future.

CHAPTER TEN

MOON, "THE FUTURE POWER PLANT"

PROFESSOR: Yash! You might have learned about power plants. Can you please say your thoughts about the power plants?

YASH: Yes Sir! During my school days, I have learned about power plants. It is the place, where we are generating electricity. We have different power plants like thermal, solar, hydro and so on. Using some techniques, we will be generating electricity.

PROFESSOR: Perfect. I thought of giving some introduction about the power plants but, you have made my job easier. Thank you.

YASH: Ok Sir.

PROFESSOR: Now Yash, Have you thought like this, that is, can the moon be turned into a power plant.

YASH: Oh! That was a crazy idea. But, how is it, possible Sir?

PROFESSOR: I will say about this research.

On March 11, 2011, Japan experienced the strongest earthquake in its recorded history, which causes Tsunami.

The Tsunami severely rippled on the infrastructure of the country. In addition to the thousands of roads, railways, homes, businesses, the tsunami also destroyed the Fukushima Daiichi Nuclear power plant.

The nuclear disaster released toxic radioactive materials into the environment and forced thousands of people to evacuate their homes and businesses. Till then, Japan relied on Nuclear reactors for 30% of its electrical power.

After this Tsunami, the Japanese started opposing nuclear energy and its power plant. This made Japanese researchers do a lot of research on alternate clean energy production.

That's when Japan's firm Shimizu Corporation proposed Luna Ring.

YASH: Luna ring?? What is it, Sir?

PROFESSOR: This adventurous plan involves building a ring of solar cells around the moon's equator.

YASH: Sir, but why did they choose the moon? Why not other planets?

PROFESSOR: Because the moon does not have an atmosphere.

It means, there will be no bad weather or clouds that could affect the efficiency of the solar panels. And, we can enjoy 24/7 continuous electricity generation from the moon.

YASH: Sir, but, how can we build a solar ring around the moon? Do we need to carry the solar cells from the earth and fix it with the help of robots?

PROFESSOR: Actually,

The circumference of the equator of the moon is 11,000 KM. To fill this circumference with solar cells, we need a massive number of solar cells to form a massive ring around the moon. So, it is not an efficient way to carry solar cells from the earth.

YASH: Sir ok, I am having an idea now.

PROFESSOR: Please tell.

YASH: Ok, we couldn't send that many solar cells to the moon, but, we can just send the materials from the earth to construct the solar cells right?

PROFESSOR: Good idea, but, that is also costly.

Instead, if we get the materials from the moon itself, that could be a perfect solution. Silicon, Aluminium and Iron can be chemically extracted from the lunar soil for the fabrication of the solar cells. Lunar soil can also be used to make concrete. Robots could play the primary role in building the lunar ring. These robots could be remotely controlled from the earth. A team of astronauts can support the robot onsight.

A concrete ring will be constructed on the Moon's equator and then, the solar panels will be placed on this concrete layer. A luna ring would initially have a width of a few hundred kilometers but could be extended up to 400 KM wide. These solar panels collect sunlight and convert it into electricity.

YASH: Oh! That's crazy. It is a perfect idea for generating electricity. But, how could we transmit the electricity from the moon, Sir?

PROFESSOR: Thank you for asking me this question. I thought of like, ok, it would be boring for you, so we can skip to the next topic.

YASH: Sir, are you kidding me? It is so interesting for me. Please continue Sir.

PROFESSOR: Thank you. I will explain this research further.

The produced electricity is transmitted through the cables to the near side of the moon.

YASH: Sir, what is the near side of the moon?

PROFESSOR: In simple words, the portion of the moon, where we can view from the earth is called the near side of the moon.

YASH: Oh! Ok Sir.

PROFESSOR: Yes.

On earth, the microwave power and laser power are converted back into electricity and it is supplied to the power grid.

Even though everything seems to be easy, there are many practical difficulties. The first one is a fund, you might have guessed already.

This project is going to cost a lot. The company needs lots of investors. On the technical side, even though the solar panels are not affected by the bad weather conditions, they must face lunar dust. The company must find a solution for this.

Now, it is 2022, Shimizu Corporation has announced that they will start the construction by 2035.

YASH: That would be another milestone in our mankind. That is impressive and awesome.

GRAPHENE, THE GAME CHANGER

YASH: Oh no! the charge on my mobile is very low. If I charge my mobile now, it will take too long to get charged.

PROFESSOR: Yash, have you ever thought of charging your mobile in 5 seconds.

YASH: Wow!!! If it happens, it will be a great thing, but, how is it, possible Sir?

PROFESSOR: I will tell you in detail about it.

If we take transportation, it could take up to 20 to 30 hours to completely charge a mid-size electric car. So, with this situation, the present electric cars won't appear to be a solution for the fuel crisis.

Now, just imagine what if we could charge our smartphones completely in 5 seconds. How about charging your cars in 30 seconds.

Fortunately, such things are technically possible. The Research and Development works are going on progress towards achieving this marvelous thing.

Someday soon, such technologies may reach regular customers. You will be surprised to know that one solution for all these is a pencil.

YASH: What??? Are you kidding me?

PROFESSOR: Yes. Let's see how?

We know that graphite in the pencil is used for writing which is made of carbon atoms. Using a pencil, let us draw a line on paper and observe it through a powerful microscope. Just assume, it can show graphite lines on the atomic scale. At this atomic scale, the structure looks like a stack of paper having many layers over the other. If we take one layer among that, it looks like a honeycomb made of many carbon atoms.

In 2004, Physicists Andre Geim and Konstantin Novoselov conducted a simple experiment using some graphite particles of pencil and tape. They placed those graphite particles on the tape. They folded the tape, separated it, and observed the graphite particles being separated. They repeated this experiment plenty of times and each time, more and more layers of graphite were separated. At the end of the experiment, they were just left with the one layer of carbon atom called Graphene.

This outstanding discovery yielded them at the Nobel Prize for Physics in 2010.

YASH: Oh! Ok. But, why graphene is so important?

PROFESSOR: Expected question.

Graphene is the strongest material discovered on earth so far. Hundreds of times stronger than steel. Even an elephant standing on it cannot break it. So, it can be used to build aircraft, space crafts, satellites, cars, motorcycles, bulletproof jackets, and so on with high durability.

Despite being stronger, this material is millions of times thinner than paper and flexible as rubber and also it is transparent.

Also, graphene is 1000 times a better conductor of electricity compared to copper. Therefore, graphene can shape the future of electronics.

In the future, we may see super slim electronic devices built using graphene. Phones, Laptops, Tablets will become as thin as paper. Just like papers, we will be able to fold these devices and carry them in our pockets.

Charging time consumed by mobile phones and laptops today is a big inconvenience. In the future, the capacitors made of graphene as mobile phone batteries could significantly reduce the charging time up to 5 seconds. Similarly, electric cars can be charged in 30 seconds using this technology.

Still, there are huge challenges associated with manufacturing graphene for such commercial purposes. However, students like you must research this, and please bring us these incredible technologies and make our dreams come true.

CHAPTER TWELVE

DEMAND SIDE MANAGEMENT

YASH: Sir, in recent times, I have thought that the consumption of electricity has been increased drastically because of the increase in usage of electrical appliances. I accept that we need electricity. But, the demand for electricity keeps on increasing. So, what do you think about it, Sir?

PROFESSOR: Your thinking is correct and I appreciate your thought at this age. There is a solution for this. Actually, there is planning called Demand Side Management.

YASH: Oh! I hope it would be interesting to hear.

PROFESSOR: I will tell you about it.

As the day begins, homes, offices, Industries, and even farmers plug in various electrical appliances. Now, the demand for electricity keeps on increasing. In the evening time, as we switch on all our lights and fans at the same time, the demand for electricity further increases and reaches a peak. Now, the demand for electricity has different patterns on the weekends or any special occasions like festivals. The demand also varies according to seasons, weather conditions, geographical locations, or lifestyles of people. So, what is the solution for this? The solution is DSM.

DSM stands for Demand Side Management. DSM is a concept that helps to better manage the demand by either reducing the electricity consumption or shifting it from Peak to Off-peak hours.

YASH: Sir, what does Peak Hour mean?

PROFESSOR: When most people consume electricity at the same time, the demand for electricity will be more. At that time, the period of the maximum demand is called the peak hour.

YASH: Ok Sir.

PROFESSOR: Now, this DSM can be done by using Comprehensive Load Research.

YASH: Sir, what does Load mean?

PROFESSOR: In simple words, an electric appliance that consumes electricity is called the load. It is a technical term in the electrical engineering.

YASH: Ok Sir.

PROFESSOR: Yes.

There is a certain protocol to perform this DSM like observing the power consumption of the load, Consumer categories, and so on. A consumer survey will be taken for performing this DSM. This all will be done by the electrical engineers.

YASH: Sir, was it implied in India?

PROFESSOR: Yes.

The concept of Demand Side Management in India is not new, but even today, it is yet to pickup because of the lack of proper metering and availability of digital records of data.

However, Demand Side Management is the critical need of the hour. It saves utilities from purchasing expensive power to meet demand. The consumer does not have to suffer power cuts, the government can deliver its promise of 24/7 power and manufacturers can have a ready market for the energy-efficient appliance.

75

CHAPTER THIRTEEN

NET ZERO

PROFESSOR: Now Yash, have you heard about Net Zero?

YASH: Net Zero! Strange! I don't know Sir.

PROFESSOR: It is related to controlling global warming.

YASH: Oh! Now I guess that completely reducing our pollution and emissions to 0% right?

PROFESSOR: Not exactly.

On hearing the name "Net Zero", we might think that Net Zero means reducing all our emissions to 0% like you.

If that is true, is it possible practically? Of course, it is happy to imagine a world that doesn't emit any greenhouse gases. But, is it possible for us to stop using fossil fuels completely?

The emissions from power plants, transportation, industries, agriculture, air conditioners, cooking, and the list go on and on. Now, is it possible to stop the emissions from all these things completely in our life?

It is not possible to stop these emissions. Then, what does this Net Zero mean?

When the earth's temperature increases, the earth is going to face horrible disasters. But, don't think that it is going to happen somewhere in the future, because it was already started. The greenhouse gases will be emitted by the burning of fossil fuels that are responsible for global warming. As we emit more greenhouse gases, the earth's temperature will keep going up. The hotter it gets, the harder it will be for humans to survive.

Now, we can define Net Zero as the balance between the number of greenhouse gases produced and the number of greenhouse gases removed. This means, if we can capture all the greenhouse gases we emit before it enters the atmosphere, then our net emissions will be zero.

YASH: Oh! That's great. So, we can emit more greenhouse gases right, because we can able to capture all the gases.

PROFESSOR: No, It doesn't mean that we can emit more greenhouse gases. Our intention must be that, we must try to reduce the emission of greenhouse gases to the maximum level.

After that also, if some greenhouse gases are emitted, then after that, we can remove it

YASH: Ok. But, how to remove the greenhouse gases we emit. Is there any special kind of device like a vacuum cleaner to clean all the unwanted gases from the atmosphere?

PROFESSOR: *Nature has a solution for this.*

During Photosynthesis, plants take in Carbon-di-oxide and give away the oxygen. So, one of the ways to remove carbon dioxide is by planting billions of trees. Afforestation is the primary solution for removing the greenhouse gases emitted in the atmosphere.

The other way is by carbon capture. This is the process of capturing carbon dioxide, transporting it, and storing it underground. It is viewed as the only practical way to achieve deep decarbonization, in the industrial sector. Companies and governments are investing more in this project. Researchers are trying hard to find a solution.

YASH: Oh! That's good. But, are countries aware of this?

PROFESSOR: You know what, actually there are some countries which took an oath that they will achieve this Net Zero within 2050. Many countries were working hard to achieve this mission possible.

YASH: Ok Sir. Sir, but, what is the relation between this pollution control and electricals?

PROFESSOR: Do you think electricals are not related to pollution and the greenhouse effect?

YASH: Probably not?

PROFESSOR: No, there is a relation between electrical and global warming. I will justify this.

We are using an enormous amount of electrical appliances in our home. From Bulb, TV, AC, and the list goes on. We all know that flow of electricity will be there along with the dissipation of the heat. If this heat dissipation is happening in one home means it's ok, but, if this happens from billions of houses from the country, then definitely, it is global warming. The population is rapidly increasing. So, the usage of electrical appliances will also increase drastically which increases global warming.

YASH: Oh! I haven't thought about it like this. Then probably, what might be the solution for controlling this Sir?

PROFESSOR: Some small initiatives and thinkings are required.

For example, If you take an old incandescent bulb, the power consumption will be more in that bulb, which causes an increase in heat dissipation. Same case for the fluorescent tube lights too. So for this, we can replace them with LED bulbs and LED tube lights as the power consumption and the heat dissipation are less. Like this, if we take some measures, we can partially able to control global warming as electrical engineers.

YASH: Oh! That's cool. Then as an electrical engineer, I can also give my contribution to the fight against the global warming.

CHAPTER FOURTEEN

CONCLUSION

The train finally reached Delhi.

YASH: Sir!!! You have opened my eyes. Frankly speaking, before speaking with you, I was not at all interested in electrical engineering. But, Your explanations of the concepts changed my thought. You didn't explain to me with any pen, paper, or blackboard, and you haven't drawn any diagrams or written anything. You just explained the concepts orally, but, I can able to visualize your explanation like a screenplay. Even though it is a train journey, you sincerely explained the concepts. Thank you so much, Sir.

PROFESSOR: Nice to hear this from you. But one thing, it is a field with a lot of complications. You must be sincere in your learning. You must also update yourselves with the latest technologies in this field. There are lot of opportunities in electrical engineering, but those opportunities will reach you depending on the skills you have developed within you after the 4 years of your study. Here is your new life. Explore it with abundant interest because "Will is the Way".

YASH: It is a great pleasure for me to meet you, Sir. We have just discussed the concepts randomly, but still, I got the confidence in myself that, I can do something in this field. I got the spark now Sir.

This is a life-changing moment for a youngster, who has chosen electrical engineering. Many youngsters have chosen electrical engineering also even electrical engineers could not able to find the right field of interest because of certain circumstances.

This book is dedicated to all aspiring electrical engineers. This book intends to trigger the interest in the field of electrical engineering and to create "The Spark" among the youngsters.

Thank you all for patiently reading this book.

www.ingramcontent.com/pod-product-compliance
Lightning Source LLC
Chambersburg PA
CBHW050758160726
48004CB00002B/609